The Ephemeral Shades of Time

OCT - 4 2021

D. R. Toi
223 Southlake Pl.
Newport News, VA 23602-8323

The Ephemeral Shades of Time

A Reflection in Poetry

By
SEAN ALI STONE

In life, there are some who stand apart,
Not because they are more alone than the rest,
But they are more deeply aware of their solitude.

They walk alone, they sleep alone,
Knowing that they are born alone and shall die alone.
Indeed, they understand that all existence is a solitary one.

Waterside Productions

Photographs provided courtesy of Harun Mehmedinovic.

Printed in the United States of America

First Printing, 2020

ISBN-13: 978-1-949001-39-6 print edition
ISBN-13: 978-1-949001-40-2 ebook edition

Waterside Productions

2055 Oxford Ave
Cardiff, CA 92007
www.waterside.com

Table of Contents

Author's Introduction

When I was young, I was told that I was too sensitive. I was the kid who did not like to be away from home for more than a few nights. I was the kid who loved poetry and classical music. I was the kid who got sick from stress and anxiety at school, then stayed home on Mondays. I was the kid who loved to read. In school, I would have been considered a nerd if I wasn't also an athlete. I suppose my ideal was closer to that of the Ancient Greeks who prized the body and mind equally, but the soul more than anything.

Yet I came of age at the end of the 20th Century, when the emphasis was on 'cool' visuals, technology, and the euphoria over capitalism's global dominance. Money and success seemed boundless, so what did *soul* matter? The battle lines had been drawn between religion and science, and science was winning the intellectual debates. Meanwhile, religion seemed increasingly inconceivable, dominated by fundamentalists and true believers. Not that I felt 'soul' was a matter that belonged to any church or clergy. In fact, I had no idea where to find my soul, except that I did not doubt its existence. And yet, unable to prove it with science, I felt stricken by the unanswered questions of *why* I was on this earth, for what purpose, and how could I ever be certain of it?

While in daily life I contorted myself, like an acrobat, trying to fit into the mold of society, I knew I never belonged. I felt like a pilgrim, passing through the world, recording its gargantuan contrasts and paradox, then storing the records in my writing, and perhaps closest to my heart, in my poetry. For I've heard it said that poetry is the language of the soul. So this is an expression of my soul, collected over twenty years, from a teenager who traveled to refugee camps in Somalia and Kenya, visited the memorials of war in Vietnam, Bosnia, and the Cambodian killing fields, landed in a war zone in Sudan, then watched the chickens come home to roost on September 11·2001. But as we have learned, that was not the end of the story.

The things I have seen and felt along the way served as signals, like a light tower on a moonless night, reminding my heart to awaken, for there must be more to this world than the entropy of death, disease and despair that we witness. We humans are treated as outcasts on our own planet, scraping for pennies from others, to pursue some semblance of material glory, all while dividing ourselves into groups worse than gangs, hating each other over political party, nationality, race, religion ... And the gulf between man and woman widens, in our inability to accurately communicate what the Beatles promised, "All we need is love." Could *love*, by way of the heart, be our link to the soul?

Through the years, my appetite for the metaphysical has only grown, as I observe the synchronicities of life reaching out to remind me daily not to surrender or give up, for there is much more to this human drama than we can imagine. After all, life has an indeterminate quality, as do our thoughts and emotions, which shift like the tides, and can never be contained by measurement. Even the orthodox must admit their moments of doubt, and the materialist must wake in the night plagued by terrors of the unknown, beyond the comprehension of data and facts. And so our poetry, like music, gives comfort in the face of the infinite. For music and poetry – the reformulation of fixed notes and words – bring us closer to the transcendent. But at that moment of seeing it … it shifts, right before our eyes. Such is the grace of this quixotic journey. It's the fuzziness of the thing that attracts me, for imagination is far more appealing than logic.

So in the reader's interpretation of these moods of two decades, I am most excited by what thoughts and feelings might arise, for my cosmic dream is to wake the soul.

The Sign of the Harbinger

Many will see me without knowing why *I am*.
My initials stand for lightning,
And like lightning, I manifest when conditions prevail.
You see the apparition, you judge what it creates –
But you cannot approach the why,
For the lightning was always there,
Though alien to our sight in its informed potential,
As stillness in its unspent truth.

And whatever the meaning,
Some magnetism has culled us to this place.
We appear, we disappear –
And yet we live out incarnations,
Ever participating in the universal desire for change.

The Birth of Poetry

In the time before the dark,
There was only light.
Till a yawning veil fell across the sky,
Separating space in night.
Leaving us in awe of the infinite shadow –
That behemoth, that monster.
But from the waning of the light,
Our world was formed. Another broken.
With enough night left to dream by.

Sine Die

It could be conceded in prophesy,
By the wisdom of elapsed time,
That I eloped from the clutches of despair
When I was rejected by my lover's arms,
And ejected unto the ether of cosmic plasmas.
The sucking of space was positively claustrophobic
To a sensuous soul, singed at the vapid touch,
Torn mercilessly by the specter of pale cloud dust.

Crushing each nerve in their chilling embrace,
The sonic rays confined, and thrilled me
In their absolute control, channeled at once
Through me, in the numb black –
So black, not a photon of light illuminated
What I saw without sight – in a future
Of light shredding through infinity to birth color,
Concluding light as the source of woe.

Had I known words, taken to oath,
I would have formed curses …
Yet I had not voice then, but a scream –
A shock of wave to pierce through a crystal veil.

Torn from my embryonic love, sliced
And scattered through the ligaments of time,
This inchoate self,
Knowing not events,
Nor form,
But the weight of dissolution.

So unleashed were the phenomena of feeling,
Tangible but for truth,
That I thought of nothing in this eternity of formation –
When light breathed life across a threshold of night;
And I, in my somnambulant endurance,
Pressed, before the invention of hands,
To hold the stuff that things are made of,
Presaging its concurrence in us – the stars.

And in us stars,
inflated by whims of atomic permutations,
Conscience first conducted froth to obedience,
Rending the waves tame in recurrence,
Submissive to the axis of creation.
The act, rightly ridiculed had it been intended,
Endeavored to rend the alien from itself,
To recover the part in its whole.

Never could I conjure such
consecrations of color's light,
Strewn by stars and sown by comet seeds,
Had it not been for a snoring mind,
Dreaming of that moment of coercion –
The alpha and omega of love.

Love Cry

In the midst of burgeoning night,
My heart softens to flames of old.
Romance is the word that decries we
Mingle, I and you: Venus' afterthought.

I wish to love you by the light of the stars,
Till our fire leaves them jealous.
Heated by the fury of a kiss,
Not even a claw's tenderness could we spare.

As long as your star calls to mine,
I will not allow your departure.
Instead, let us dance to our silent drum,
Let our tongues scorn restraint.

Even let the sun turn day from night,
Our hearts shine brighter than any light.

To the Mystery Woman

To a free spirit,
A wandering soul,
Dancing through your days:

Find your place,
In it will be peace,
And air enough to sail.

You are a princess,
With gold ether to fuel volcanoes' lust,
Brimming like the swell of music.

You are no goddess,
Surpassing nobility by humility,
And the insecurity of a hunted gazelle.

But in my eyes,
No one shall ever compare
To le petit oiseau.

For each flaw,
I see only humanity.
And in that,
You can never go wrong.

Whispering Winds
of Woe

The sun illuminates the world,
Surrounding us with its gold hue,
But I envision nothing
Beyond your ancient eyes.

Each breath captivating my heart,
In trepidation that it may be
Your last to fall on me.

Together for now, in this moment
Of tumultuous silence.
I resist your departure,
I reach for your flesh,
I retain only air,
Wherein your shadow lives
For me, forevermore.

I have surrendered my soul,
Delayed the slightest reparation.
An image remains in my heart,
So emptiness can reign my mind.

If I commanded any true power,
I would love nevermore.

Temporary Sight for a Blind Man

Each day was like night,
Of unconscious grazing,
Stumbling without form,
Until I grasped …
My meaninglessness.

And then you entered,
Intending where each foot trod.
Your scent consecrated the air.
And in your eyes,
Mine softened to the dark.
I breathe just to know you live still.

Without you in this world,
Gone, too, am I.

What of Love?

When love is at your side,
The horizon doesn't seem so far.
The earth rises; the sun never bows.
Its rays stretch without blinding;
Even the rain is trifling.

When love is at your back,
The angels no longer cry
When the storms grow fierce;
Now they laugh their tears
At our mellow halos.

When love's breeze flows through you,
The night no longer draws.
The stealthy sprites lose their chance
To beckon from the wild.
Even scowls belong to jest.

But beware!
When love's no longer there,
How merciless the rain falls,
How menacing the sun stands,
And snarls wrought on quivering lips.

The Mirror

The mirror stands before me.
Another stares back – a synchronicity?
He has neither name nor soul.
Still, the hollow man resembles me.
Even probing his eyes
Forbids difference between us
But in the fantasy of his rage,
He would break through that cage.
And still a coward,
All I would do to not be devoured,
Is to avert my gaze –
I try, tepidly, to respect his fury,
But in such moments, sight grows feint.
His visage, construed with a thousand faces,
Gradually molds and interlaces,
As the shifting skin recedes
Until only the eyes are perceived.
Those pilfering crystals,
Adamant.
Within, the boy is done, fully grown.
It is now I cast my heart in stone.

In the Depths of Solitude

(Dedicated to Tupac Shakur)

That's what Pac once spoke on;
Now he's my only friend.
It's cold having a ghost for company.
But nobody ever bothered to ask.

I'm in my depths of solitude,
The twisted caverns of the mind,
Where the world's just a cold shoulder,
Brushing me aside.

I used to be lonely,
Now I'm just alone.
There ain't no one to reach to;
Wish walls could talk,
Instead of keeping you in place,
'Till concrete offers redemption.

Even the dreams are stifled,
Choked in the humid air,
Caught up in dry tears
Over the death of dreams begot by
Misery's father – reality,
Its twin cousins – pain and joy,
And its children – the profane.

Like living for the sake of it,
I'm in my solitude,
Looking over my shoulder,
Looking back to my child's face.
Yeah, I recognize a smile ...
But now I live in the shallow solitude.

Remembering who isn't cursed,
Are those not blessed.

Memory of Memories

Like dew evaporating with the morn,
My heart shines into corridors locked.
A simple prayer serves to whisk me away,
Back to memories, stocked.

Like rain flagging my sail,
I picture a child idling.
A glimpse in her eyes never called me,
But now this ode to passing, and I cried.

Like grass clinging at the wind,
I imagine a boy defying the world.
He cursed his lot, having never sinned,
Yet stood helpless, on the verge of mortal fall.

Like the birth of a flower,
I echo the song of days.
Never content with limited powers,
I strive to end our amnesia,
By reaching for the bird-havens
That embody all He loves.

A Glimmer of Light

I remember the twirl of the turnstile,
Before the crowd's cheer announced the first pitch.

I remember the flutter of cream curtains
When you left mother by the door.

I remember your whiskey-stained breath,
While you coerced my innocence.

I remember the flex of your pale ankle
Before the tension of your first plié.

I remember the furrow splitting your back,
Turned from my outstretched palm.

I remember the sweat on your upper lip
As the charred roof fell on our childhood home.

I remember the vinegar taste in my nose,
Smote by the boulder destined for you.

I remember the kiss of the blood sky
Blessing our rain-starved wheat.

I remember the flurry of wind-whipped leaves,
Waving after the departing plane.

I remember the base of your taut spine,
Coiled round the blasted mortar shell.

I remember you waving the black banner,
Even as my warrior's face was porcupined by arrows.

I remember the hunched back of the busboy,
Scurrying for the last ship across town.

I remember the crack of the armada's bark,
Sunk behind a soupy mask at dawn.

I remember your hysterical eyes,
Spitting into my wanting cup.

I remember the twitch of your nose,
At the command of "I love her."

I remember the turn of your thumb,
When you sentenced me, eternally.

I remember the stain on the concrete
That could never be cleaned.

I remember the smirk of your lip
Before swallowing the hemlock.

I remember the phone call you promised
That never came.

I remember it all,
But I prefer to forgive.

Sarajevo, Bosnia

I saw a cemetery once ...
Crooked tombstones lamely eroding,
Crosses sustaining the unfenced yard;
How they twisted away from heaven.
A few flowers,
(Red, white, blue)
Flavoring the blank sky.
The grass is not greener on the other side,
If there's grass at all, save the dirt.
And all around this plot of despoiled souls,
Roaring highways drown out their cries,
Too many to be heard,
Amidst the misplaced names ...
In lovely Sarajevo.

Civil War

Awash in the infected room,
The mosquito trap as sanctuary,
I elevate myself from the net,
Hesitant at the dirt underfoot.

I stall on the porch of the world,
Just beyond the overgrown realms
Of penetrating jungle, survival's burden;
I envision a desolate tomorrow.

The camp rouses outside my sight,
Moans from the dead and nearing,
I lunch on breakfast, fresh from the can;
Tuna pacifying my afflicted heart.

Where else would I be but here?
Like some vague thought of Jupiter,
The presence of people snows my recollection,
While I set in this camp, with the future.

Isolated Earth

"He must have looked up at an unfamiliar sky through frightening leaves and shivered as he found what a grotesque thing a rose is and how raw the sunlight was upon the scarcely created grass."

— F. Scott Fitzgerald, <u>The Great Gatsby</u>

No matter that I may search for a friend in the pen,
The pad no longer seems so receptive.
There are times when the creative bile flows,
untempered,
But those echoes of axioms fade with the sun.
Intrusive while inquisitive,
Not within my own heart,
But permeating the paper itself:
Another blank extension.

I'm afraid there is nothing left to write,
The propositions exhausted, abandoning the fight.

Suffocated by the pervasive air,
my existence in question,
Out there.
The windows speak to multitudes beyond me:
Within finds its end.

Awghw! Thousands of miles from the closest friend,
Stunted in all dimensions by verbs
That turn my hopes to woes.

My mind tears,
My heart cracks,
My will breaks.

Surviving is not living.
One breath before another,
And I shall last to imagine one other,
Flee this body coldly,
Never to return so boldly.

African Games

The last gust of poetry burst through his veins,
Clocking another hour.
The boys in the street no longer cared,
Consumed in their docile games,
Kicking cans through the dirt,
Their bare bellies swollen
For want of supper.

The afternoon light reflecting the saltwater
Tugging at his lids.
The boys retreating now,
Kicking sparkles of earth
Between their crumpled sneakers.
Their skin, inflamed and dyed by the sun,
Cried deficiency, drying with the day.

They made their departure,
Without evidence or clue,
But he remained to weep them to sleep,
At the final call to prayer,
When their only friend had set,
And the boys' can was hijacked by rats.

The Rain

As I fell upon a journey,
Just one amongst the pack,
Tears wrested from my eyes,
And epochs from my days:
Time, eternal, dissolved in knots,
Naught more nor less than resolved.
Where I am not,
That is where I long to be.

I swam the gulf,
Its waters seeping from my eyes,
Everything with its sting,
The salt, the sand, the wind.
There was no end to this journey,
Flashing images of my unattainable,
Stealing memories of my future,
Tearing confidence from my heart.

The ignorance gone,
I emerged from my self,
Walked into the night,
Sat aside the rest.

Perched in isolation,
I coalesce in absence:
With the whiteness of a wall.
Until I faded from the night.

The rain continues its descent,
I shall never feel a tap,
All passed through me;
All there was, will be,
This journey:
My heart is sick of sorrow.
Fatigue bids me wake.

The journey raped me of bliss.
That, I never had.

The Wise Gaze of Nothingness

Gold mists of the dawn,
Swaying my sweet moon away,
Burn fire someplace else;
I enjoy my unconscious lay.

Dear rapture of sleep upon our weary form,
Can we ever possess you in this life?
Your tender respect for our person,
Dutifully liberating our self-possession.

Yet I dread your presence,
Your bewildering gaze,
Mincing precious hours,
Seeping visions from our blood.

I sing your praise,
For I could not exist without you,
Though chilled by your aplomb,
Leaving me vulnerable to the world.

We can only imagine the globe
While seduced by your rapture.
Better leave me die out here
Alone, but ever awake.

Your tempting stories stir my wonder
Though feigning rest, while together
Traveling through emptiness of mind,
Articulate as the seduction of night.

You would afflict my gentle soul,
By phantasmal arousals
Unlocking my cryptic unconscious; or worse,
Taunt my sparse peace, with negligent promise.

Yet I forgive your embassy,
For in my ignorance, I wake
Abandoning the realms you offered,
When I was free of the woes of time.

The Birth, The Death

The tedium of hours' tired song,
My heart breathes again,
Releasing that feint glow of past,
Replacing it with the reign of jet fumes.

Casting shadows far from home,
My heart wakes with the moon,
And I remember what it is: alone.
Envying the little owl outside my catacomb.

Beautiful night saved my life,
The sun charred my will.
But I stand renewed before the task,
Blood strengthened fast to lay still.

Day may be where others thrive,
But night is what keeps me alive.

Out of Somalia

"It is better to conquer yourself than to win a thousand battles. Then the victory is yours. It cannot be taken from you, not by angels or by demons, heaven or hell."

— Buddha

So then I returned, and still no more happy.
Sure, I hooted and gawked at the passing lights
Stimulating each city – Addis, LA,
Just like that first taste of the Big Apple.

Back then, I'd just lie on the roof and stare
At the stars getting high in that sky.
There was no life for me, out there
In the desert night.

But how wrong was I to ask for consolation at home?
When loneliness is etched in the heart,
There shall it rest,
The fiercest battle raging in this breast.

And now here I was, lodged in a doorway,
Watching tears depart the skies of home,
Wistfully recalling that last day in Hargeisa,
When I pressed at the cusp of the dancing rain.

Rain paved my road, drew the curtains,
Repelling this unwelcome guest.
So where am I, this stranger to all places,
Never escaping that which is within ...

There is one path to bear this grief,
This dagger in the heart,
This dulling of the senses,
And that is to want for nothing, need of none.

This organ that grows cold will never know sorrow,
And its paradox of pleasure.
But that is the price to be paid,
Mimicking voices of jubilee as I quietly harden,
Descending into strength,
Repellent though it may seem.

Show me another way out of Somalia,
And I will let you into the light of my heart.

Falling Star

When you see a star rumbling,
Soothe it with *souciant* prayers.

When you see that star fire,
Ease its velocity by striding aside.

When you see that star tumble,
Adjust your axis to brace it.

When you see the star crashing,
Tender the earth with fertile care.

But once you've said goodbye to the fallen star,
At least you remain ...

2001: A Grain of Sand on the Shores of Time

Once upon a dream, the dancer rises,
Like a whirlwind cast out a desert night,
Formed from the ocean of ourselves,
Stealing across forbidden skies,
Painting an ode to light,
Inviting our souls to song ...

I scent the coarse snare of time
Raking a sentimental heart,
Till in relent, it shreds,
Surging from spine to fingernail.
I hear the dull yawn of the dead
Centuries, quaking to retrieve me.

Can we dissuade this century from its end?
Or coax this giant from a graveyard's peace?
At the end of the American Century ...
An age of doubt, to distil our disillusion.

Loneliness can't describe the city –
It's the pure density of the thing.
The buildings ally against you.
Built on the backs of slaves, crushed by Caesars ...
For a cup of coffee.

But when the cities turn to dust,
The sea above still belongs to us.

The Harbinger

I am the harbinger of the world to come,
Prophet of a bygone age.
Those who come after will wonder at
What follows ...
Never daring to ask.

They'll see corpses strewn out 'cross
Highways of encrusted scorn –
What was a man, now a spectacle
For all who dare perceive.
And those who smiled melted away
With the ease of a gold-crusted cask.

"Behold, what shall be,"
Quoth the passing Roman,
Pondering a sacrifice, posed in vain,
A debt collected in pounds of flesh,
Before he cloaks those mutilated hopes
With white robes; a benediction.

"It cannot go on!"
Thundered the howling wind,
When it smeared with its breath
That frail puss of flesh.

What forgeries lie in wait,
When we commence on this road's task –
Better to be the man bearing the cross,
The man who extinguished himself willfully,
Than the poor, headless John,
Exterminated along the road to prophesy ...

The Wrath of "God"

It was a beautiful day in paradise,
With rainbows dabbing the sky,
When the first rockets sunk into the sand.

Lovers and children were at play on silver beaches,
When distant wounds ripped fresh.

The gush of the ocean's tide competed only
With the wave of light on stagnant autos,
While desert winds eviscerated tank tracks.

Our clouds, assuredly clear and white, are
Frail as the haunted smoke of a city alight.

Babylon was lit on-fire,
Broadcast and scripted for TV,
But it was a beautiful day in paradise.

Empty Skies

The skies have shrunk
Since the blue dome soared
With cream-puff platforms, from
Whence we witness God's domain.

The skies have hushed
Since the healthy squawk
Of red tails wavered,
And hawks turned to cold chrome.

The skies have fallen,
Since stars painted the veil
And dust twisted our view,
When lights' flash striated the night.

The skies have soared
Since man took flight
In glistening metal tubes ...
What heavens shall we envision;
Or shall we become?

A World Apart

Picture the roasting house of feast.
Here comes the little one, armed with silver spoon,
While the smiling masks pantomime behind glass,
Hidden by fluorescents of monotonous tone.

Now, a family cozying 'round a dying flame,
Few morsels of grain lying in wait,
As the famine resigns to hunger,
As the desert stalks the night.

Just as we ran, simmering in the oven,
Over mint grass, delighting in acorn trees,
So do they, the forgotten ones,
Jest and muse, earning their lives' worth,
Making much of disappeared youth,
As their joy traces the desolate earth.

A morsel of food would never satisfy
What God has stripped of his lambs.
We speak of trite justice,
While our words turn to air,
Echoing to the grave.

The New Alphabet

A E I O U
Stick these words to me; watch them come back to you.

K P Y L Q
Can't blame "US" for a horror or two.

J C N S V
Just tell yourself: Que sera sera, and
there's nothing left to see.

H D R F T
Wish you'd see how power cor-
rupts when you think you're free.

G B W M Z
And while you laughed, they stole what gave you breath.

… X …
A symptom of our unrest.

The Wrath of "God" (II)

And when paradise burns,
Placid-lipped spectators, those statues of men,
Squawk and flee without repudiation.
Seas tumbling through vacant skulls,
Thoughts writhing to regain ...

Vampires once abounded the night,
In mansions tucked on-high,
From the poor agitation of despair.

Those palm-oiled hills now aflame,
Washing out the blood of cows ...
Left too long to pasture.

Will you weep when you hear the whine,
Writhing from without – your phantom twin –
At the nihilistic edge of creation.

What tears warranted?
For a mock heaven?
By whose decree?

Not even a ghetto's stench could match
What paradise burns, worse than a garbage pale,
From the fury in the repressed heart,
From the cities, absconded to blight.

As we once watched
From make-believe houses,
So too might we one day know
The holy wrath of 'shock and awe'.

The suns burn hotter with the torches,
But on fire comes water,
So that we may build again.

The Forgotten Soldier

(For My Grandfather)

This is dedicated to you, the many,
On a now turgid battlefield, away.
You who felt both compassion and scorn,
Who knew that joy and pain could taste the same.

You left your hearts at home for keeping,
With your bodies still, effortlessly far.
You gave your ideals to glory,
But you will never again share that word
With those who believed in it.

You're forever changed these days,
Overcome by an untimely gain.
But in your passing,
What will become of you,
Who lost the life we claim to prize ...

Another shade upon a field,
Shattered by a fleeting enemy,
Counted not so different than yourself.

Back home, self-pity mourns
The name on a stone
That reminds of eternal youth.

Pity our tears,
And those who question why you are gone;
Lost to forgotten wars
For things that now seem inconsequent ...
You were your father's son,
Yet, his hour, too, has come.

So we heed your singular, echoing call,
Played in salute upon the deathless wind.

Why.

"I want the Moon."
– Albert Camus, <u>Caligula</u>

Why do they ask incessantly?
As though they do not know,
Why left long ago.
Being a question was hard,
So it took the facile turn,
And concluded itself:
To know, simply, we must go.

To fight, for cause without reason,
There's reason still.
To fight for a sin-stained nation,
Penitent through vague chauvinism.

But why, do you still inquire?
Because I wish to cry,
Genuine floods, from haunted eyes,
Pursued by scarlet sin.

Then these tears I weep
Over the dead
Will never again be the tears
Of a lunatic: looking for the moon.

Anthropocentrism

Shhhhh!
Can you hear it?

Swish-Swash
The troubled leaf abandoned by the limb.

Swish-Swash
The ocean's scream at the sand's stir.

Swish-Swash
The wind that titillates the hearth.

Swish-Swash
Passing nanoseconds, decaying a lifetime.

Swish-Swash
The gods, frantic in their abstinent plea.

Swish-Swash
The perturbed scent rarely carried this far.

Tick-Tock
Bliss demands we ignore how our kings are gone.

The Shadowland

Sometimes, to sleep is to wake.
To dream is to behold the cosmos.
To close one's eyes is to witness infinity,
And shut out the moving pictures of mortality.

What opens the door is not elemental, but essential,
Transporting us in place – an image –
Mocking our mental captions
By a cordoning thought ...
To behold the residue of death,
The hewn odors of decay,
The morbid consequence of life.

By penetrating, pursuing loss to its deepest core,
To hide within its unbridled walls of
Chipped stone and unrequited hopes;
To inhale its stinking sulfurous breath,
Is to know what matter suffers.
The worm conquers ...

Until you have reached beyond the bone,
The intemperate truth,
To break free, morphed
By the lucidity of the gallows.

What animates flesh-worn space,
Not mere shadows but signs,
That the body can be mutant,
The form transcended,
And where there is one transformation,
Alchemy prevails in love.

An Induction to Pleasure

No less cryptic than toxic,
Limp fingers stretched aimlessly to confirm
That earth be set aright in its bearing;

For a fluid hour, silence begat
A viscous fleet of jarring perturbations
Out teething mouths, after
Ponderous outbursts but a thought before,

Ensconced in this cave of vibration,
Each soft stir an ecstatic crush
Across my numbed skin,
While I listen to the abstract parables of time,
Told to the lie of our deceptive ears, and I

Might be meandering to beg
Illusions from the past,
Now distant and petty,
Like a feeble old shoe sunk in soot –

No more real than the fleeting future,
Left unattended, to percolate

With hands converting the Grail
Behind a peerless laugh,
At the mockery of flesh –
Engrossed by the anatomy of sweat,
Germinating from the infinity
Of an infinitesimal drop –
Imparted and embossed,
But by the drug!

Why, Pt. II (We Die ...)

Why does half pine for love,
While the other snidely turns aside?
Why does half yearn for a quick demise,
And the other jealously clings to be alive?

Why should I be afraid to die
When countless others have passed before?

Why can't I sleep when night falls,
Then shut my eyes to day?
Conflict amidst turmoil,
The anarchy of peace.
More than a riddle,
I'm a double-breasted beast.

Why should I be afraid to die
When I precede countless more?

That smile you see,
From the far beyond:
There's pity in the lips,
Garbling their confession;
Remorse in the teeth
Gleaming before the bite.
Joy in the tongue,
That spews from the gut;
Pain in the cheeks,
Tired of dutiful flexing;
Longing in the breath,
Waiting for a blessing;
Resolution in the twins sparkling,
Already envisioning the hereafter.
That irascible grin,
Fizzing on the face,
Only wants to kiss, then shudder.

Why suffer, I query in a breath,
And in the other ....

Why not?

To the Late Night Hours

I love swapping white lies
With wide-eyed, meretricious girls
In the post-midnight hours;
When the champagne clinks chill to harder fare,
And memories of last night's hangover are swallowed
With a throb in the throat and a kiss on sticky lips.

I love the inconsequential words we shout,
Competing with the drone, inglorious beat
Rattling its cacophony against our inner-ear,
As we sneak off with girls we're forced to adore
Within the hopes of a drawn-out, heavy sigh.

I love the way their fingers cradle
Emptying chalets of beer and wine,
While they vainly seduce love,
To be grasped in the other hand,
Until, at least, *one* empties.

I love the taste of their wet mouths
At the moment we reach for that hesitant embrace
Tying ourselves by obvious words,
Glimpsing their deceits, their tales,
At last breaking through, to silence.

I love the still of the dawn's approach,
On the nights when we depart alone
Into the quiet of the morning's lull,
Unscathed by vague, distant songs of night's tempest:
Blowing, blowing us apart,
Carrying us a breath away.

Dust in the Wind

I never played the piano so well
As my fingers danced along
The rim of your flower,
Learning to play by the sound
Of your moans,
Tuning to my fingertips.

Your body was perfection,
At the end of a long carafe,
Suppliant to my grasp,
Even when your tongue fought
With a bitter caress.

And still, there is no end to this need.
With a hand wrapped cross your waist,
My lips teased your neck,
While my eyes wandered to the women
Sliding their hips to the parading sax.

And I wonder, how many men
You tasted with that tongue?
As many as you have adored, would it
Be any different, were it one,
Or an infinite sum?
Why should your love for them be any less
On this lonely night of longing?

I could never own you.
But should I claim you this night,
Your dress would fall away
As your breasts cling to mine,
Warmed by the heat
Of a stirred pulse.

But sensing the conquest of your will,
You pulled free into the night,
Fleeing the wanton play,
In search of my pursuit,
That I prove some greater devotion.

How long could I pursue you,
Through how many trails
Cast by the scent of luckless
Men, discarded like beasts,
For the demands of an hour?

And if we two shall never entwine,
Then what did it matter
That you glimpsed my fantasy this night?
Was our imagined love-making
Any less, that you did not act
To consecrate the transgression?

As you disintegrate now, into the tick
Of a clock upon my bureau,
I ponder your thoughts in the sun's
Drawing gaze, and where you might be,
Upon the blue sphere.

Soaring like dust upon the receding waters,
In the embrace of some lover?
Or searching within the well
Of your soul, ever thirsting
To drink ...

Night at Dawn

A dissembling shadow rises on the corner,
Adapting to the city's shade.

A traveler wanders through
Gates of squandered night.

A woman's face steers crooked lips
From the brake of cars.

An inebriated brain stumbles
At a solicitous overture.

A honk stirs restless sleep,
Uninvited to the last call.

An intrepid stranger retreats from an offering,
Parting the sacred night,
At dawn.

The Pilgrim's Chorus

It is the Pilgrim's Song we hear
Drifting from th'ancient wood,
Rising through sun-soaked valleys,
'Cross the cool timber of moist mornings
When we wake to wander
The earth, unfolding.

And while my heart can beat a hundred years,
It still recalls the shattered bits it has collected:
Piecing together a stranger's fate
As he quivered at the swift on-set
Of rain, and an ominous land,
Till he could no longer tell which port
Launched his embarkation.

It is the Pilgrim's Song that rings each tear-ridden night
He looks back across infinite space at time
And recalls the myths of lands once crossed;
A woman left unfilled by his desire,
Another love borne in the depth of his absence,
And untapped
Before his fast-fleeing heart.

In the race for gain, through lands undreamed,
He smiles, bitter at the rising sun
And remembers that ephemeral truth –
What morning welcomes, night soon shuns.
But upon *this* land, at this eternal moment,
The Pilgrim's Song tunes and does not sound ...

Destiny's Fate

My life is an elevator,
In which I am not.
I see myself from without
But do not inhabit therein.

I am stuck in the core,
Of this nicely packed 'Sean',
Willing for some way out,
As I ascend my skin.

The floor has been set,
The sky draws me forth,
There's no retreat here,
No pause without a stop.

My anxious eyes seek proof
In mock images' worth,
At the doors' overture,
With a smile that's mine to fake.

The Eternal Recurrence

Plunged into the foreclosed future,
Perceiving the imperceptible to describe this
dis-charge.

Wading on perilous ground, the night oddly
comforting,
Steadying us from this tiresome ploy,
A charade through the bedecked glow of light;
Our waking hours twisting minds
In worship of the economy of *being*.

Neither seconds nor hours describe our transfinite
existence
As we meagerly want, but for want of life,
We eat and sleep and love till only the desiderata
remain.

What horrors would the light bring should the pur-
ple, sunless sky
Return to comport us round Atlas' quickening
globe –
Twirling dance of passage, from morning, noon to old
age
And re-birth!

Night be praised!

Blessed honesty, mask this heavy swath of sun,
Paramount of energy-binding dealer in visions,
As we scream in silence that we may live another
day –
Eat, sleep, love and feel wanted, lest we were …
If not, then deny me, and I cease this ephemeral day,
Like a man crying out, do not forsake –
Give me life, here and hereafter!
Before the bones and the blood ebb, without decay.

But here comes the rain we drink, the shelter we seek,
And the night beckons us to yearn for
Apollo's distant, deprived star.
What memories prolong nights' journey to day?
Were I not an immortal man, born unto moist clay,
I would not dare recall your great future,
Nor desire its recovery –

For I have traveled along that starry plane
Of glittering, effulgent blacks –
And colors! Such as you have not yet seen.

I am before it now, hearing the call of a distant home,
But waiting still, that I may offer some transfinite
comfort
To this returning hearth of clay ...
And yet be human.

Then it came, for it always was, and ever will be,
Though we did not know what we knew,
In that moment of eternal prose
When our universe was born,
Pregnant with ambition to bear itself anew
In the mind of man,
To be fantastically adored ...

So I beg, why desire what once was had
Before you have been,
Should you never live to know it?
For you, too, shall fly across an infinite space,
Intentions eternal, without resource to reclaim it ...
And like me, you shall be left with
Nothing but a question
And a distant memory of a sun,
And only the sun – precious, random star ...

I am

Where am I?
Am I in my brain
When I claim
I am here?

Am I in my fingers,
When I grace your hand,
In a silent greeting
Of recognition?

Am I in my gut,
When I welcome this meal
Into my hearth,
Though barely tasted?

Am I in my breath
When I suck at air
Grasping to vitalize
My racing heart?

Am I in my eyes
When I register a spark
In your eyes, hinting at a time
Before we knew of space?

Now I'm in the sky
Surrendering cities like sandcastles,
No greater than ants, but in transit
Where am I?

Now I am nine,
Sucked in the memory
Of water overwhelming,
As I strive against the tide.

And when I die,
You speak my name,
I am on your lips ...
So where am I?

My Mind:
A Question

How strange to look 'out' at the world;
To perceive it elsewhere,
But to be not 'in' it.

Bound by the limit of my mind,
The depths of my fascinated senses,
Situating my psyche to perceive.

Conceiving,
to be bound by such thoughts,
The color of these dreams,
As proof that I have never seen,
Never imagined, nor reflected,
Except that it was 'I' who did.

But to abandon this I,
To become 'you',
Would I not still be me?

Would it not, alas,
Be my mind's scheme to
Bring the universe to fruition?

Whether within, or of it,
Before, then beyond,
I cleave to be here,
While it remains there –
And should we two ever merge,
How could I go beyond 'me'?

A Face in the Crowd

Who are you?
These thousand and one faces
I swear I've seen before ...
And for what they are to me, here –
I have.

A flush of discrete faces,
A life's story flickering between the flash of light,
But neon glow can'ever elaborate
Where personality fails to show –
In the chaos of slapping palms,
Sweating bodies beating out the bass,
Pursuing a mad monochromatic voice –

But for one, I would like to dance with you.
But for one, I am captivated by desire.
And still, who are you?
Are you as pleasant as your high,
As inane as that smirk,
I wonder at these repeating faces,
Seen on a myriad flashing nights.

Are all equally unknown
As that one I see least?
While my eyes pursue you
Searching, to reassure the presence
Of one face I cannot see –
Most alien, most alone –
My own.

Wilderness

Ten Years in the Wilderness,
and look what I've become,
from the days of my fast pursuits,
lusting for my creations, to make way
on some marveled, silken screen.

Spurred by the urgency of endings,
my mind wandered in a great wild,
beyond the concrete bounds
tread by peripatetic fiends,
whilst grasping at moments
to be transported by cares,
if ever they were caught.

Back then, the catch was the game,
awed by each new creature – apparitions
to entice me down a crevice
of such dense yarn,
that only memory might portend
the lugubrious den's denouement.
Till then, neither man nor beast
existed in that wilderness,
to light my road, my concoction;

but like a monk at matins,
I whispered prayers to alight my ears
with companionship,
letting creation know,
I was on my way.

But what could I know of my "way",
without an audience to perceive it,
as I ventured on imperceptible streets,
and erected shrines to remake
my imagined procession –
a vagabond's course, whilst
cooling my mind with the cooing
of birds, and flowers' teasing.

I stirred my pride, fancying
ancient gods admired my half-constructed
archetypes, gleaned not from them,
but of a future architect in starry-fields,
arousing the kaleidoscopic sky
tempting our spirits to lift it,
charting our delights, though never fixed,
in the wandering of an aeon,
in the wink of a babe's dream –
forlorn years in the minds of men,
along an unvarnished path,
unfamiliar, yet remembered by the traveler.

What will one remark in witnessing
my creation's form, once standing,
before world-weary sight?

What matter murmurs,
when a universe of matter
has conspired with time,
to bring these matters to light,
not in commemoration of an ideal,
but in consideration of inspiration,
woven like the forgotten paths,
between the gyroscope of stars,
by eyes that could divine.

The Last Breath

Be, then hold ~
Parading over tide's dormant states,
Awaiting a chance to perspire,
To execrate this stasis in one crest!
In one treble of motion,
To unleash a word,
And conclude this trembling,
To awaken ...

Wings stretched beyond the horizon,
Perilous, tumbling through the ever –
Lapsing spaces, replacing the void;
Fill it with the distending wind,
Of the breath in my lungs –
The beat of this tour of devotion.

Having traveled across the Aeon,
This sanguine heart begs repose,
To gather the courage
'For it leaps once more,

To the end of the peril,
To the dawn of the tumult,
To the absolution awaiting
This great transfiguration ...
At a birth, reborn.

Nostalgia

When I was a kid,
Fridays were the peak.
Only baseball cards could compare
With the roll of movie trailers
Before glimpsing the main attraction.

No male desire could compare
To the thrill of a chase,
Hunting through husky oaks
Before my friends negated the tag
And captured the flag.

When I was a kid,
Saturdays were bliss,
Without the delay of homework,
Or the interruption of recess,
To splurge and be free.

The neon lights of the city danced,
But when mom called it a night,
Bedtime stories made tomorrow
Less distant in its incentive
Of another game to be had.

When I was a kid,
Sundays were mercurial,
Torn between fancies
Of week's end,
And dreams of what the next
Might hold in store.

But a toy store might ease
The unease of transition
Because there's nothing like taking
Action figures in hand,
Then mounting a tale of your own.

When I was a kid,
Mondays were dread,
The long haul of the week ahead,
If only the order of days
Could be rearranged.

But there was no need for escape
When mom and dad were home
To hear the stories
Of what I'd learned that day,
And what I would one day explore.

A Princess, Of the World

A princess, kept in the ruins of her castle,
She asks not what she reveals in rehearsing
For this ever penultimate debut –
To appear before the caustic crowd.

Rendering them once more her subjects;
In each of them, their vanity mutes,
'cept when she prattles through a play.
Though jesting, her poised projection
Conveys more truth
Than words could parlay.

For she is holy keeper of a mirthful world,
Where glory grays with abandon.
And though bedazzling in ivory,
To go unseen would rust her sheen,
Were it not for the rainbow streaking
Through the prism of her ravenous soul.

And so she dwells in her castle,
Chiseled by the praise of a fawning parade.
Vainglorious would be her pursuit,
Were she not a princess to the world,
And a reflection of its aspirant cool.

Epigenesis

Ever remember the eminent command
That you are here to serve ...
God or Devil.
Which do you choose?

To serve God is to be one with all;
To serve devils, all with one.
Which is to say, do you choose
Your self alone, or your true self?

In time you learn, alone and one
Are the same, through distinct prisms.
In you, find all. And honor that star,
By serving it well.
For the battle came and went with you –
In your primordial heart –
The heart of the watcher
Gazing into the endless night.

Through that dark
You longed to see.
For being alone, aware

Amidst sleeping darkness,
You were tempted to rest.
But for fear of never waking,
You crafted the living-dream
By looking to spaces within.

And to know this is to remember,
To confront your greatest fear –
That infinite black,
Hidden still deep within,
That inspired you to create this.
And you still do,
In the eternal now of knowing,
And seeing!

Moment by moment, you are the dream
In the eye of your Godhead,
Ever desiring to desire,
To distract yourself from that dark source
When you believed you were alone (all one) –
So infinitely singular
That you created light
To dazzle yourself into *believing*
That you had never been alone.
But you have always been, ever-present
With yourself – one as all.

But in doubting my oneness,
I disbelieved you.
So long was the black hole my home,
I knew no end to me,

Till I imagined a star,
That you and I might exist,
As you leapt from that dream,
Catapulted cross an encroaching sphere
In quest of darkness
To slay and conquer
On behalf of light's eternal right.

Culling wisdom from clouds
Of Seder's dust
We form breath to whisper,
An echo of prayer
To cease destiny's tear,
Torn from lips
Screaming for dreams of color.

We journey through the lands of Nod,
To wake the dark from its slumber.

Ends of the Earth

Returning to the ground I left long hence,
A lapse on the shores of time,
I stare blankly, great distances off,
Ever beyond my vigilant gaze.

Anticipating their swift descent,
Monstrous forces thriving,
I seek no more to wander,
Doubtful of a longed-for asylum.

Night urgently ascends my mind,
Though I know its sojourn brief.
How long 'for I part these untimely hours,
With only the moon as my steer.

Softly now, 'ere the darkness comes;
But am I to hasten to some far-off place,
Wherefore – not here?
The pale barge beckons.

I am resolute:
Winds may stir,
But bamboo merely sways.
As tides churn sand in its place.

I adopt the yogi's stance ...
This endless sky forever my shelter,
This vast earth eternally my land,
This small planet permanently my home.

One Love

Do you know the nights I dreamed,
And in the random, broken images
Of stained glass memories,
Apprehended little of the dreams?

Do you know the days I wandered,
Chatting up the merry female form,
Chancing a glimpse at hidden delights,
Searching the valley of love-making?

Do you know the nights I cried,
Empty promises on insincere lips,
Praying for a genuine word,
For reconciliation with the divine?

Do you know the days I reached
For my love, the one I never saw,
Swearing I was god's gift to her,
While she had wanted no rewards?

Do you know the nights I pursued
Every breath, a desire
For momentary detention,
To fill the vacuous hold?

Do you know the days I emptied
Myself of all emotion,
Expecting to never meet you,
Or wrap you in my arms?

Do you know the nights I listened
For the spirit seeking its voice,
In endless anticipation,
To one day greet you?

Do you know the day I smiled
In hearing you through your words,
And feeling that warm cool
In my chest, the retinue ...

Top of the World

Have you been to the top of the world,
And if so, would you accompany me?

Sinners call me a saint,
And to saints, I'm a sinner.
But without you,
I don't know what I'd be.

A captive to your heart,
You would wash my feet if I asked,
And for you, I hold the space
For the quicksilver of our love to flow.

You provoke me to the tip of implosion
Then contain me
With the calm of a finger's touch,
To retrain our souls to trust,
For we have all been wounded
On the jagged slopes of caring too much.

Then the sickness of separation
Engorges the belly,
Choking the restrained voice
That wishes to say, "Don't go."

Distending in breaks of tangled affairs,
We play with tendrils of bad faith
To reach the edge of doubt in waves,
Then reignite the shelter of our cocoon.

But even if we never reach
Those tops at the edge of sight,
Beyond foot's length to reach,
We can soar to that plane
With our imagined wings –
Inspired by faith in each another.

For in the challenge of our love,
We find that diffuse light without source.

Child of the Light

Who are you? Taught to deny the thoughts tempting
From behind your eyes – and call them *dreams*,
Despoilers of sleep's lure to forbidden realms.

You speak of imaginings as you would
Wandering vagabonds out to creep,
Toying with your still sense of certainty.

Yet you know not why you live,
Entombed in mortal needs of air and liquid delight.
When asked what you believe, you dare not speak it,
Not even to breathe the name of the infinite.

Then, of course, you vie for power to mock
Covert gates of sex and death,
In lands you envy to control.

But you, fantasy of your own design,
Could never be, without a blessing.
So what force permits you, in the
absence of that self-made self?

Alas, you have awakened
Trembling eyes from self-induced trance,
From a time when fear confronted feel-
ings you swore to never share.

Here I woke you from this spell. But I am you.
And were that not true, you'd no more understand me
Than hear a tree fall in an empty wood.

For in the realm of the conscious,
One and one make one.
Or are you not eternal,
Oh child of darkness,
Blinded by its light.

Imagine ...

Imagine a world where hugs are greetings,
Where words are honored,
Because we're genuinely happy to share this world
With each other.

Imagine a world where contracts are expansions,
And agreements are oral,
Because goods are traded between friends
Until all share in the wealth.

Imagine a world where you're not seen as a commodity,
Because millions won't follow soulless posers,
Ignoring the cues of social engineers,
For we are all creators.

Imagine a world where people do what's right,
By trusting their intuition,
No matter what their leaders
And laws tell them to.

Imagine a world where feelings are valued,
Enough to be expressed
Instead of scoffed at, because
In the eyes of the young is the heart of the mature.

Imagine a world where the sickness in our souls
Is treated as carefully
As a doctor working in the ER,
Knowing that healing only happens inside.

Imagine a world where imagination is honored,
And society looks at its own shadows,
Rather than projecting them onto others ...
We'd all be set free.

Imagine if we stopped trying to force the world
The way we want it to be,
And started to love our life
Just the way it is.

Imagine if every child were told
That they are enough;
Instead of competing for more,
We'd make room for everyone.

Imagine a world where you have nothing to prove
And to breathe is the miracle,
So people smile at your sight,
To know you are welcome, and thanks, for being here.

Where Are We Going?

With honed grace,
The ducks trace an invisible line,
Following the leader,
Stirring the lake of its rest ...
Where are they going?

Daffodils disassemble in the
Subtle breeze of portent,
Beckoning the sky to defy
The ply of gravity ...
Where are they going?

A bee eases into a flower's lip
Busy in its ubiquitous pursuit
Of stamina for the hive,
Obsequious to mother's design ...
Where is it going?

Light dances on the waves,
Tempered by the frequency of water,
Ever seeking its release
From this recapitulation of day ...
Where is it going?

A songbird's call tunes us
From our lax hypnosis,
To decode the unknown verse,
By the curiosity of its delight ...
Where is it going?

We lay on the lemon grass,
Subdued by spectacles until,
Tempted by feats and folly, a promise:
To ordain us with purpose ...
But where are we going?

Until the End of Time

I am the heat in the night.
The cold in the light.
Strong as grass,
Frail as oak.

Let me be your blanket,
Let me be your shield,
Let me be your spirit,
Until, until, until I am healed.

Wisdom beyond words, power beyond time.
Beings lost, found in a deluge of permutation.
Memory, forget me.
We, but hearts trembling in the dark.

Let me be your blanket,
Let me be your shield,
Let me be your spirit,
Until, until, until we are healed.

Realize the unheard song.
Truth in union: the abyss.
Life rinses in death when grown complacent.
Wisdom rhymes without word, tuned without sight.

Let me be your blanket,
Let me be your shield,
Let me be your spirit,
Until, until, until we feel.

Vigorous freedom questing
In youth's wandering daze,
Chart your soul's crest
Higher than the deepest within.

Let me be your blanket,
Let me be your shield,
Let me be your spirit,
Until, until, until we unite.

Should I live,
Too deep to be forgot,
Recollect me with a twinkle.
And lay my piece aside.
Until, until, until ....

Sean Ali Stone is a filmmaker, author, poet, and speaker. He has been a spiritual seeker all his life, studying meditation and global religious traditions since his father took him to India, Nepal and Tibet at 10 years old. Stone has hosted the interview show *Buzzsaw* for the LipTV and Gaia, the news program *Watching the Hawks* for RT, and the podcast *InnerViews* for Vokal Now. Stone has acted in films such as *JFK*, *The Doors*, *Savages*, *Night Walk* and *Fury of the Fist and the Golden Fleece*. He is the director of films such as *Greystone Park* and the documentaries *A Century of War*, *Hollywood, D.C.*, and *MetaHuman* with Deepak Chopra.

A student of history at Princeton University and Oxford, he has published the non-fiction history book *New World Order*. In 2020 he released his second book, *Desiderata: A Cosmic Fairy Tale by Ali*, on Audible. *Desiderata* will be available in 2021 in print form, accompanied by a Wisdom Deck.

Some of the poems from *The Ephemeral Shades of Time* are featured in the spoken-word poetry album *Alien Spirit* created by Stone and acclaimed musician Michel Huygen (formerly of the band Neuronium). *Alien Spirit* is now available on Spotify and iTunes.

To find Sean's work, please visit his website www.SeanStone.info

Made in the USA
Middletown, DE
01 October 2021